Written &
Wayne Lynch

Whose NOSE Is This?

Whitecap Books
Vancouver/Toronto

Edited by Elizabeth McLean
Interior design by Warren Clark
Cover design by Peter Cocking and Maxine Lea
Photographs by Wayne Lynch

Printed and bound in Canada

Canadian Cataloguing in Publication Data

Lynch, Wayne.
    Whose nose is this?
    Includes index

    ISBN 1-55285-174-5

    1. Animals—Identification—Juvenile literature 2. Nose–Juvenile
literature. I. Title.
QL947.L96 2001   j591.4   C00-911560-9

The publisher acknowledges the support of the Canada Council for the Arts and the Cultural Services Branch of the Government of British Columbia for our publishing program. We acknowledge the financial support of the Government of Canada through the Book Industry Development Program for our publishing activities.

People have big noses and small noses, but all of them look much the same.

Our noses drip, they sneeze, they sniff, and they snore. Your nose tells you if your lunch will taste good, or if your sneakers need washing.

Wild animals have all kinds of funny noses. Some animal noses are furry and have long whiskers, some are big and floppy, and some are flat and scaly. See if you can figure out who owns the noses in this book.

The whisker spots on my upper lip are unique, just as your fingerprints are different from anyone else's. My nose is covered with scars from fighting with other animals. For food, I hunt zebras, wildebeests, and gazelles. I sneak up close, then jump on them and grab on with my sharp claws and long teeth.

Who am I?

3

You probably guessed that I am a male lion, the king of beasts. I live mainly in Africa, but also in a small part of India. I usually live with other lions in a group called a pride.

There may be 40 female lions and their cubs in a single pride. A large pride can protect a bigger hunting area, where there is more food. The females do most of the hunting for me and the cubs.

A lion usually kills an animal by biting its throat, so that it cannot breathe.

You can see from the dry scaly skin on my nose that I am very old. In fact, I might live to be over a hundred. I am also very large, and can weigh as much as your entire family — so I move slowly. Although I spend most of my time on land, I am a good swimmer. When I'm tired, I like to wallow in a mud hole with other old-timers.

Who am I?

I am a giant tortoise, and I live on the Galapagos Islands in the tropical Pacific Ocean. I use my nose to sniff out the juiciest plants, even the prickly fruits and pads of cactus.

Blood-sucking ticks often bite through my tough, scaly skin. To prevent this, I let small birds eat the ticks off my skin. When I want the birds to help me, I raise myself as tall as I can on my legs, and stretch my neck out so the birds can search everywhere for the juicy fat ticks.

A mother tortoise lays eggs as big as a tennis ball, and she buries them in a deep hole.

I am a master mouse-catcher. I find mice under the snow by listening for them with my big ears. When I hear one, I leap into the air, and pin it to the ground with my front paws. I also like to eat the scraps that wolves, bears, and mountain lions leave behind when they kill other animals. I use my sensitive nose to locate these tasty meals.

Who am I?

I am a red fox, the most widespread carnivore, or meat eater, in the world. I live in deserts, prairies, mountains, forests, and farmlands all across North America, Europe, and Asia.

Not all red foxes have red fur. Some have black fur tipped with white, and are called silver foxes. Others have brown and tan fur, and are called cross foxes. But we're all part of the red fox family.

A male fox is called a dog, and a female is called a vixen.

My nose is big and floppy. When I snore, my nose jiggles. Most of the time, I live far out in the ocean where I hunt for food. My favorite foods are fish and slippery squid. Often, I dive so deep that the water is completely black. I can hold my breath and stay underwater for over two hours.

Who am I?

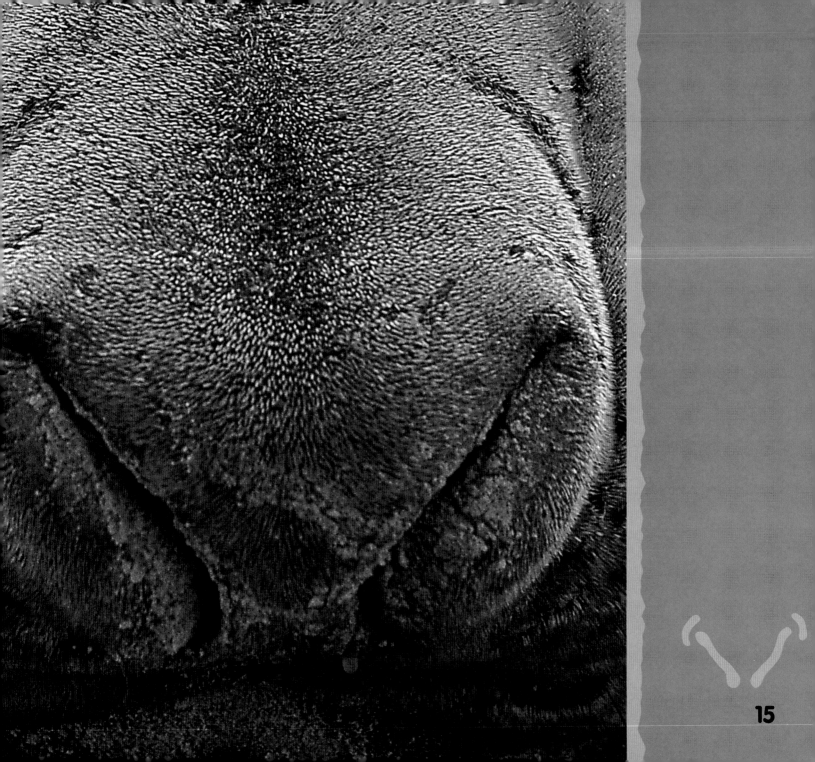

I am a male elephant seal, the largest seal in the world. When I am fully grown, I am longer and heavier than a small car. I live in the cold waters around Antarctica.

Every summer, I come ashore to warm up and molt my old skin. Hundreds of us may pack together on the same beach, which we often share with penguins.

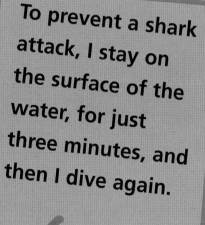

To prevent a shark attack, I stay on the surface of the water, for just three minutes, and then I dive again.

Most birds can't smell very well. But I can. When I am flying, I can easily sniff a dead animal, even when it is hidden under leaves on the forest floor. I am Nature's original skinhead. Because I have a bare head, less food sticks to my face when I eat, so I stay cleaner. My bare head also gets redder when I am hungry or angry.

Who am I?

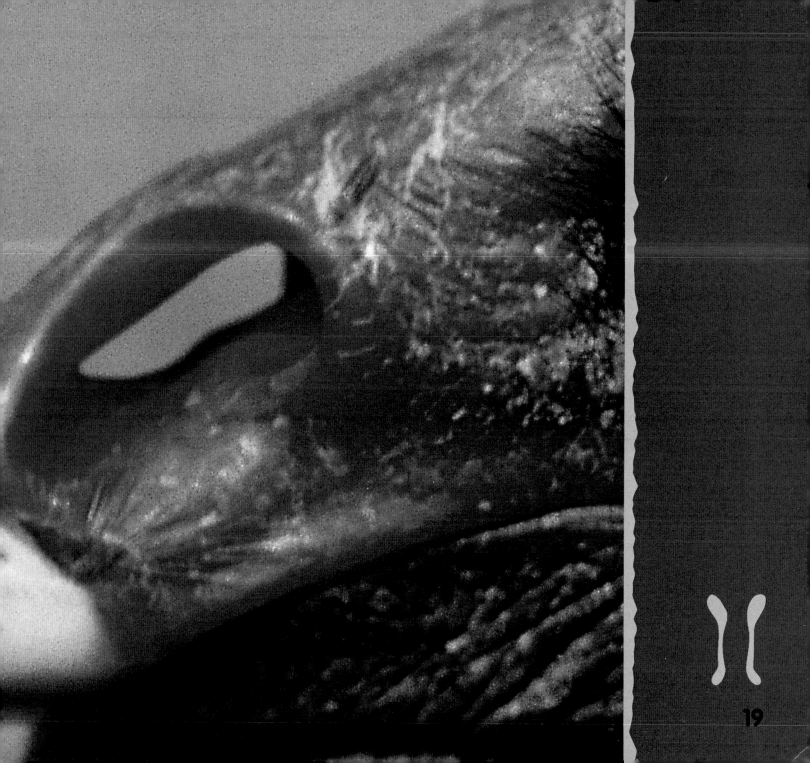

I am a turkey vulture, and I live in the forests and prairies of North and South America. To find my food, I soar all day long on my large black wings. I have blunt claws and weak feet, so I can't hunt well. Instead, I feed on animals that are already dead.

I am one of Nature's best recyclers. I can eat rotting food that would make other animals sick without getting sick myself.

Baby vultures vomit on predators to scare them away.

I use my droopy, fuzzy nose to sniff twigs, leaves, and other plants to decide if I want to eat them. In the summer, I like to swim in deep lakes to escape from biting mosquitoes and blackflies. In the water, I can stay cool, and I can also dive for salty water lilies and other underwater plants — some of my favorite foods.

Who am I?

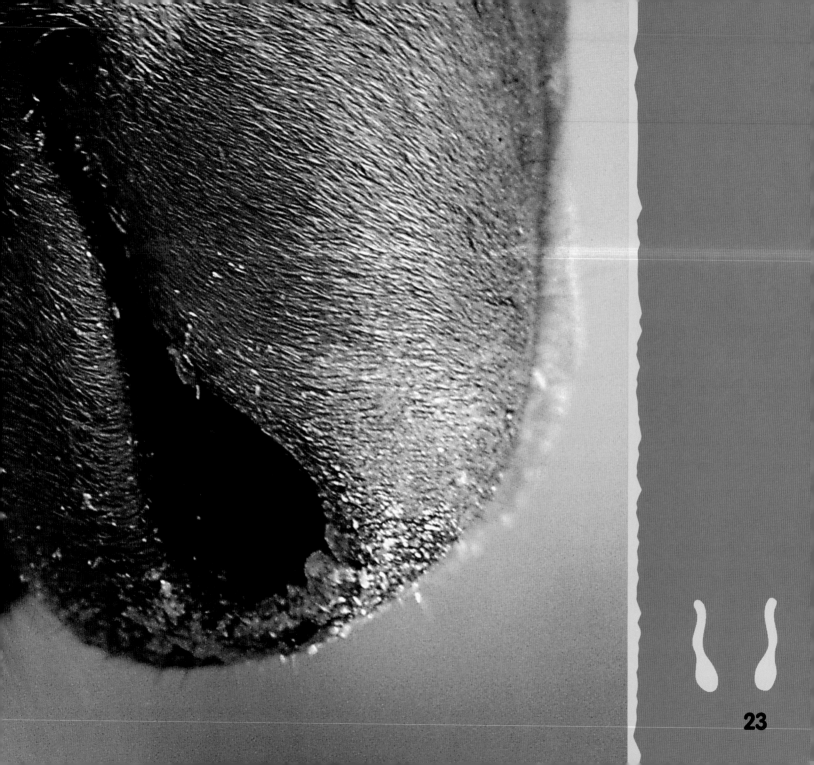

I am a moose, and I live in the northern forests of North America, Europe, and Russia. I am the largest deer in the world. My shoulders are taller than those of a horse.

In winter, I use my long legs to wade through deep snow. Hungry wolves sometimes try to attack me, but I use my sharp front hooves to defend myself.

The huge antlers on a bull moose fall off in winter, and a new set grows each summer.

I eat a very simple diet: leaves, leaves, and more leaves. The leaves I like the most grow on eucalyptus (*you-kuh-**lip**-tuss*) trees, and smell like cough medicine. I eat so many that even my fur smells like medicine. I spend most of my life sleeping in trees. Up there, I am safe from dingoes — wild dogs — and big lizards that might want to eat me.

Who am I?

I am a koala, and I live in the eucalyptus forests of eastern Australia. Like the kangaroo, I am a special kind of mammal called a marsupial (*mar-**soo**-pea-ell*). Marsupials raise their babies in a pouch on the mother's stomach.

A baby koala eats its mother's poop, to get the bacteria it will need to digest the tough leaves.

A baby koala stays in the pouch until it is six months old. After that, it rides on its mother's back until it is strong enough to climb by itself.

Index